Why nat
WOMEN
Look So
Good

Understanding and Meeting a
Woman's Deepest Needs

Bill Perkins

AudioInk Publishing

How many flowers fail in the Wood—
Or perish from the Hill—
Without the privilege to know
That they are beautiful—
Emily Dickinson
1862

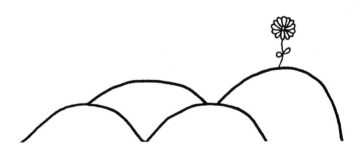

Published by AudioInk Publishing
 P.O. Box 1775
 Issaquah, WA 98075

Artwork by Robert Falcone
Distributed by AudioInk Publishing
Cover and Interior Design by AudioInk Publishing

Perkins, Bill.

Why Naked Women Look So Good: Understanding and Meeting a Woman's Deepest Needs

p. cm.

PCN/ LCCN: 2013905378

ISBN: 978-1-61339-457-1

1. RELIGION / Christian Life / Love & Marriage

2. RELIGION / Christian Life / Men's Issues 3. RELIGION / Christian Life / Relationships

For further information contact AudioInk Publishing +14255266480 or email support@AudioInk.com

For Cindy

You're Beautiful

CONTENTS

PREFACE

A Midnight Problem

This book was birthed on a sultry Friday night in south Texas while I was turning on my sprinklers. Because of an extended drought, the city only allowed grass watering between midnight and six in the morning. It did little to affect my life, though, since I'm a night owl.

As I walked out of my house and across my backyard, I noticed light coming from my neighbor's home and wondered, *why are they up so late?* Hoping to find out, I approached the fence and looked through a gap in the wooden slats. I expected to see a few people playing cards or watching TV. Instead I saw a beautiful woman talking on the phone. No big deal—if she had been dressed. But she wasn't.

My eyes locked. Adrenaline and dopamine drenched my brain, triggering pleasure and excitement.

Suddenly I had a flashback. I was a kid, playing on the swing set in my backyard in Roswell, New

1

Mexico. As I swung up and down under a star-filled sky, I noticed a light turn on in my sister's bedroom twenty feet away. A moment later, one of her friends, a senior in high school, walked in front of the window and began undressing. She stood there, naked, for only a second, and then lowered the blinds.

On that balmy night in Texas, I wasn't a kid. I was a thirty-year-old pastor with a gorgeous wife and two sons . . . and . . . and . . . and I thought, *What am I doing?*

I tore myself away from the fence and staggered to my back door, curious why the form of a human body—a nude woman—would affect me so powerfully. A question, oddly enough, I had never considered.

As I contemplated this question, it gave birth to a troubling thought. It wasn't that I had violated a neighbor's privacy. Instead, I was troubled by the problem I now faced. And by problem, I mean a serious problem. At midnight, twenty-four hours later, I would water my lawn. I would water it again the following night and the night after. Every night throughout the drought it would need to be watered. And my beautiful neighbor, whom I could watch with more secrecy than a face behind a mask, enjoyed talking on the phone at night, in the nude, shades up, lights on. I had only looked once. But I knew temptation would stalk me night after night in my own backyard.

I had a *serious* problem.[1]

By nature, I'm an all-or-nothing guy. When focused, I'm a laser, all my attention directed to the task at hand. Facing a problem this serious—a problem

I knew could ruin my family and destroy my budding ministry—I committed to learn all I could about sexual purity. I read every book I could find on the subject. I studied the Bible, gleaning life-changing insights. I spoke with experts—therapists, doctors, professors, and ministers. I met with married and single men in small groups. I surveyed thousands of men and women, Christian and non-Christian.

All this I did to answer one essential question: *How could men best enjoy their wives and remain sexually pure?* In the process, I discovered principles that have not only helped my wife and me, but have helped men and women around the world, giving them hope that healthy marriages and sexual purity are not simply lofty, far-off goals, but a realistic, attainable, day-to-day lifestyle that begins today—*right now.*[2]

As the title of this book suggests, we will examine this topic by answering the question: Why do naked women look so good? The reason I approach it in this way is because I believe:

Lifting the magnetism between a man and a woman to the high and holy place God designed it to occupy, transforms a man's life—and marriage.

The journey through all eight chapters of this book leads to life transformation. This is true because:

***each answer to the question,
why do naked women look so good,
also reveals a woman's fundamental need
and helps a man know how to meet that need.***

3

What this means is that each chapter is organized into three parts. The first part provides one reason why naked women look so good. The second part identifies what need this reveals in your wife. And in the third part, I suggest some exercises you can put into practice that will help you meet this need.

Each exercise should be tried for at least a week and up to a month. The idea is for you to see the positive benefits and continue the practice for the rest of your life. If you don't think you'd be able to make that kind of a commitment, try it for a shorter period. If it works, keep practicing it until it stops working.

The final chapter of the book is a bit different than most you've probably read. You'll join me in a chariot ride that will give insight into how you can control your fears and passions as you allow Christ to direct your life and strengthen your marriage.

By the end of this book, my hope is that you will have discovered not only why naked women look so good, but how the sexual energy generated by your wife's beauty will help you love her better.

Chapter 1

A MYSTERY

The evening I first saw my wife naked, I beheld heaven. Nothing in creation compared with the wonder of her body. Shortly after our honeymoon, I suggested we institute a no-clothing policy in our apartment, when we were alone. Being the modest type, she declined. Despite my repeated pleas, she refused to run, or even walk around our place naked. I simply couldn't see enough of her. I remember feeling as though I should cover my eyes when she stepped out of the shower or changed clothes. But I wanted to look. I wanted to stare.

Modern culture sends an unmistakable message when it comes to female beauty. Through every medium, whether advertisements, movies, magazines, or the Internet, we're bombarded with sexualized images of women. Tragically, this

reduces women to consumable items and disposable products. In a world driven by consumerism, nothing is sacred that sells. And because a woman's body sells, images of women bait shoppers to buy everything from cars and clothes to cosmetics and food.

At the same time, the dominant social force of our time, secular humanism, strips the mystery away from beauty. It teaches that men are attracted to women because of natural selection. If men didn't find women attractive, it reasons, they wouldn't reproduce, and our species would die. While that could be part of the explanation, taken alone it reduces the attraction between a man and a woman to a purely biological, animalistic instinct, which it isn't.

Ask the poets, artists, and songwriters of each generation. Or ask someone who, even once in their lifetime, has fallen in love. Beauty, love, attraction— none of it can simply be chalked up to chemical firings in our brain. There is more here than accidental evolutionary development, the random collision of molecules. God carefully crafted sexuality, creating men to find women attractive, to desire their beauty, to pursue their love.

The book of Proverbs addresses the magnetism between a man and a woman. Agur, the son of Jekah, described four things too wonderful to understand. One of them was how a man loves a woman (Proverbs 30:19). Even that ancient sage couldn't decipher the electricity between lovers. That's because:

*There is something mysterious
stitched into the heart of a man
that draws him to a woman.*

It's like sleep, for example. Did you know that scientists don't fully understand why humans require sleep?[3] Researchers have discovered what happens when we sleep. They understand what occurs when we are sleep deprived. They even know the numerous benefits of sleep. But nobody can explain why humans must sleep.[4]

Similarly, no one can fully comprehend the magnetism between a man and a woman. God has designed something wonderful that cannot be reasoned and defies understanding. If, like a mathematical formula, it could be understood, there would be no mystery. And without mystery, there is no wonder.

So one answer to the question, why do naked women look so good, is simply that it is one of God's mysteries.

WOMEN NEED TO BE VIEWED AS WONDERFUL

A number of years ago I visited the Sistine Chapel in Rome. While I had seen pictures of Michelangelo's paintings on the domed ceiling, what I saw with my own eyes astonished me. Working from scaffolding high above the floor, Michelangelo dedicated four years of his life to painting some of the best pictorial images of all time. He created nine scenes of biblical characters drawn from the book of Genesis. These images displayed his mastery and understanding of human anatomy and movement, and they changed the course of painting in the Western world.

As I gazed at these masterpieces, I felt a sense of awe. I wanted to visually inspect every inch so I could appreciate the brilliance of a man who so powerfully told God's story.

In that way I am superior to a fly. That tiny insect could buzz around the Sistine Chapel and even land on Michelangelo's paintings and not perceive their beauty.

Unfortunately, I'm like that fly when I don't recognize an even greater wonder—my wife. When she disrobes, I'm in the presence of God's final creation . . . his masterpiece. Yet, if I pass her by without a sense of awe, I am a fly.

We must reject the fly mentality of indifference and view our wives with awe. This is the first thought and action we must master because *our wives need us to view them with wonderment.*

TREAT YOUR WIFE WITH WONDER

The damage done to women by our culture is devastating. At age thirteen, 53 percent of American girls are "unhappy with their bodies." This grows to 78 percent by the time they reach seventeen.[5] This unhappiness persists throughout adulthood. You've likely heard it in your wife's negative comments about her body.

Your wife needs to see you look at her with wonder. She needs to catch you gazing with awe at her face, eyes, hair, arms, legs, and breasts.

So how can you build this into your life? While it might be easy to speak the words, it's essential to truly think the thoughts, because it is only by thought-transformation that our attitudes, beliefs, and feelings change. This is crucial if your words of affirmation are going to be heartfelt and honest.

Such advice isn't just thinking positive and hoping for the best. Recent scientific evidence demonstrates that changing what you think actually changes your brain.[6] In the context of a relationship, this has enormous implications.

Here's what happens from a scientific perspective. Your brain is composed of countless memory imprints formed over the course of your lifetime. These imprints look like  leafless trees with branches reaching in every direction. The way you think about your wife is literally imprinted into your brain. What this means is that the ways you have thought about her in the past are the ways you will likely think about her in the future.

The good news is your memory imprints are not fixed. They can be changed by replacing negative thoughts with positive ones.

Here's an example: if you notice yourself thinking about how your wife squeezes the tube of toothpaste from the middle, leaving it looking like a snake digesting three gerbils, immediately stop yourself. Then begin thinking about how she kisses you in the morning when you wake up or massages your back at night as you fall asleep. If you do this every time you think about your tube of toothpaste, you'll eventually stop thinking negatively. Instead, you will remember your wife's kisses and soft touches.

While this is a silly example, the goal is to replace every negative thought you have with a positive one. By doing this, you will literally be etching a new imprint into your brain. And because you will no longer occupy your time with negative thoughts, the old imprint will slowly vanish. Branches of your memory tree will disappear.

This is important because what you think affects how you feel. Each time you think a negative thought, your brain signals your body to release toxins into your blood system. These produce poisonous emotions, like fear, bitterness, anxiety, rage, anger, and jealousy. And every time you think a positive thought, your body releases life-giving chemicals that produce positive feelings. Feelings like love, hope, and joy.

Negative Thoughts = Toxic Feelings
Positive Thoughts = Hopeful Feelings

So how do you put this into practice? Here are two ideas that will transform your thoughts and actions as you live them out.

- First, every time you think of your wife, thank God for something wonderful about her. Fill your mind with ways you find her mysterious.[7]
- Second, translate what you're thinking into what you're saying. Verbalize your thoughts to your wife at least once daily. Mention to her that she is God's "final" creation. Use the word "wonder" when speaking of her beauty.

I encourage you to practice these two exercises for at least a week. They will require mental focus as you derail negative thoughts about your wife and replace them with positive ones. But as you internalize this process, you will begin to notice a shift in how you think and feel. And she'll know it too.

Why do these exercises work? Because you're embracing the mystery of your wife's beauty, feeding your heart and mind with edifying thoughts and emotions, filling her emotional love bank[8] with words of praise, and aligning with God's purpose for your marriage. In short, you are liberating God's love and power into your life and marriage.[9]

The mystery of your wife's naked beauty is an invisible force that draws you to her. But just because a woman's body is shrouded in mystery doesn't mean we can't glean more by examining this topic. In fact, you might already know the second reason why naked women look so good. Read on and let's see if you do.

Review

- ❏ **Why naked women look so good:** It's a mystery.
- ❏ **What need this reveals in your wife:** She needs to be viewed with wonder.
- ❏ **How you should act:** Think of your wife as God's greatest wonder and verbalize those thoughts often.

Chapter 2

HIDDEN BEAUTY

As I stand in a bookstore, my eyes secretly caress the cover of *Sports Illustrated*. It shows the face and figure of the female who won its annual competition. I conspiratorially glance to my left and right down the aisles, searching for a face I recognize, fearful someone I don't know will know who I am.

While most men could openly view this magazine, I must guard what I'm seen doing because I'm a Christian author. I don't want anyone to catch *me* peeking at *this* edition of *Sports Illustrated*.

As you might have guessed, I was checking out the *Sports Illustrated Canine Swimsuit Edition.* Every year that copy of the magazine outsells all others. Men buy it so they can salivate over the lascivious cover and expandable centerfold. They know it is filled with dozens of photos of dogs, all of them incredibly sexy and salacious. Golden Retrievers sporting dental floss thongs, Pit Bulls lying on a sandy Caribbean beach, sensually eying the camera, Chihuahuas frolicking in the frothy water, their tongues scandalously wagging at the sand.

Of course, you've never seen that edition (nor have I). The images that wink at us from magazines, entice us from televisions, and lure us from computers are not of dogs. Men don't scour the Internet for pictures of naked animals. And it's never a dog, however exotic, that summons men across a bookstore to a magazine cover. Advertisers know dogs are good for selling dog food, leashes, and wireless fences. But a competition for sexy dogs—is there such an animal?—will never empty the magazine racks like a bikini competition among beautiful young women. Have you ever wondered why? The answer provides another reason why naked women look so good.

NAKED DOGS

Over the years, I've owned eight dogs: a German Shepherd, four Cocker Spaniels, a Great Dane, a Chihuahua, and a Goldendoodle. The most unique of the pack was the Great Dane, a 185-pound horse of a dog.

When I walked him around the block, I felt like the Pied Piper, tailed by curious neighbors. Adults wanted to pet his massive black head. Children wanted to hop on his back and take him for a ride.[10] No one could believe his size. When people asked his name, I'd say,

"He's Big."

"He sure is," they would say. "But what's his name?" "He's Big," I would reply, trying to conceal a smile.

They would furrow their brow and look at me skeptically.

"That's his name," I would continue with a laugh. "Big."

I anticipated such conversations when I chose his name, hoping to create my own version of Bud Abbott and Lou Costello's classic routine, "Who's on First?"[11]

Beyond his size, what amazed me most about Big was his gregarious nature and how quickly we bonded. Anyone who has ever had a dog understands how they become part of the family. They ride in our cars, sleep in our beds, listen to us talk, and comfort us when we're down.

When my boys were younger, they occasionally dressed Big. They would slip red Nike shorts over his hind legs and a white sweatshirt over his front legs. Next they would secure a hat to his head and sunglasses over his snout.

While Big looked cute dressed up—maybe comical is a better description—he didn't need shorts and a sweatshirt because of this simple fact: dogs can't be naked. Nor can any animal. Think about it for a moment. No one has ever been shocked to see a dog strolling down the street without pants and shirt. And no police officer would ever ticket a dog for indecent exposure.

Nothing can be naked in the same way people are naked. Not trees, rocks, dogs, or dolphins. As men, we're not curious about the nakedness of animals. We don't peek up a bird's feathers while it flies overhead, hoping for an erotic glance. We don't check out a dog's butt as it pads by wagging its tail.

But humans are different, women particularly so. The thing is, while women can be naked, they seldom are. The women we see every day, whether at work or the grocery store, all wear clothes. And these clothes hide from male eyes what they most want to see.

Tim Allen, the comedian and television personality, told the story about the first time he saw a picture of a naked woman. He said, "In a way, the picture was both frightening and reassuring. I realized for the first time that, dumb as it sounds, all women are naked under their clothes. . . . That discovery made me distrust all women forever: they're hiding this! They have this power and I didn't even know it. It's just under their clothes!"[12]

Allen raises an issue most men identify with. Namely, how can women walk around every day, hiding something so wonderful? And how can they pretend they don't know what they're doing?

I find his comments amusing, but also helpful. Amusing because they openly express what most men always knew but never fully realized. Helpful because they reveal the second reason naked women look so good.

> *Men desire what is beautiful,*
> *and hidden from their eyes.*

Men are aroused by the seen *and* the hidden. Looking back, I'm glad Cindy didn't walk around our apartment undressed. Her modesty prevented me from getting accustomed to seeing her nude body. This enhanced her beauty and increased her sexual power.

On the flip side, like other women, she likes to highlight her good looks with makeup and clothes that complement her best features and catch my eye. This too is a mystery. Men are visually driven and women are propelled to beautify themselves.[13] We are opposite ends of two magnets.

WOMEN NEED TO BE AFFIRMED

We now know that the second reason naked women look so good is because men seldom see them that way. With this in mind, it makes sense a woman would enjoy enticing a man by hiding her most alluring features. This truth surfaces an important need in a woman: *she needs her husband to affirm her when she tries to look sexy.* For example, most women need their husband to ogle them when they're scantily dressed. I realize "ogle" isn't a word that's used much but it's the perfect word here. It means to stare flirtatiously or amorously.[14] If a husband ignores his skimpily dressed wife or acts like he's seen it a thousand times, she'll feel devalued and hurt. A woman needs his eyes to sparkle when she's wearing something sexy.

Consider what you've just learned. Previously, when your wife wore sexy clothes, you may have thought it was all about you. Now you know she also plays an important role. She wants you to crave her. *She needs you to find her attractive—and she needs you to tell her.* When she does her best to look sexy, you must do your best to give your full attention, shower her with words of affirmation, and offer her gentle touches. By doing so, both of you will be loving one another—she by looking sexy, and you by praising her beauty.

The magnetism men feel when they see naked beauty, that sensual urge— the surge of adrenaline, dopamine, and endorphins— isn't only given for a man's gratification, but to be channeled by a man to love his wife.

For this reason, allow the sexual energy you feel for your wife to drive you to more frequently praise her sexiness.

While the Bible exhorts women to dress modestly in public (1 Timothy 2:9), it doesn't say this applies to how a woman dresses in the bedroom—or in the rest of her home. And since men enjoy seeing what's partially hidden, it makes sense for you to encourage your wife to visit the women's lingerie department of her favorite store . . . or give her a gift card at a store that specializes in intimate clothing. Help her cover her secrets with clothes that entice.

As I mentioned before, when she looks sexy, praise her. But praise more than her good looks. Praise her willingness to demonstrate her love. Praise her every time she dresses well, not just when she's wearing lingerie. Remember, she's looking sexy for you . . . so tell her you've noticed and it turns you on.

PRAISE YOUR WIFE'S SEXINESS

Here's another two-fold challenge:

- First, think about this for the next 24 hours: *The more I praise my wife, the more confident she will feel; and the more confident she feels, the more she will highlight and uncover her hidden beauty.*
- Second, whenever you notice your wife trying to look sexy, speak words of praise.

A woman has great power over a man because of his sex drive, which is only heightened by a wife who has learned the secret of suggestive concealment. This sexual power energizes a woman and enables her to more freely meet her husband's sexual needs.

Her sexual power, however, is drained each time her husband fails to notice her when she's trying to look attractive. The opposite is equally true. You empower your wife when you praise her beauty. You charge her femininity when you notice her with excitement.

Yes, naked women look so good because men seldom see them that way. But there's a third reason that touches a man's heart.

Review

- **Why naked women look so good:** Their nudity reveals what is hidden and beautiful.
- **What need this reveals in your wife:** She needs to be affirmed when she's sexy.
- **How you should act:** Praise your wife when she dresses or acts sexy.

COMPANIONSHIP

The moment I saw Cynthia Russell, I melted. Like a chocolate bar exposed to the sun, I liquefied, flowing across my desk, dripping onto the floor. Realizing how silly I must have looked, I pulled myself together and sat up in my seat. My heart pounded like a manic drummer as I anticipated a glance of her flashing brown eyes. If she looked my way, I would smile and she would blush. We would quickly avert our eyes, too embarrassed to maintain a gaze.

We were in the third grade.

During lunch, I wondered about Cynthia's favorite food. While sleeping, I dreamed of walking hand-in-hand with her. On my way to school, nervousness consumed me as I thought about seeing her. In her presence, not a syllable fell from my lips. In fact, the entire school year I never talked to young Cynthia. On those few occasions when I worked up the courage to speak, my jaw froze. This rendered my tongue as immovable as . . . well, an ice tongue. I did, however, carve

a heart into my desk with
an arrow shot through it,
framing the script: B+C.

I felt as though my
life would be empty as a
shell without her.

Of course, our union
was not to be. But all was
not lost. That experience
taught me I had a hole in my heart that could only
be filled by the girl of my dreams (a girl, coincidently,
named Cynthia).

Adam had no such childhood experience to teach
him what I discovered in the third grade. Had he spent
his adolescence in a classroom full of cute girls or had
he gone to a school where he and his friends competed
for girlfriends, he would have learned this lesson, like
me. But Adam didn't have such experiences to reveal
his need for a companion.

Fortunately for Adam, God noticed his condition
(he actually created him that way). After each creative
day, God looked at what he had made and announced:
"It is good." Following the sixth and final day, during
which he made Adam, God declared his work "very
good" (Genesis 1:31). That's what makes his statement
about Adam's aloneness so profound. The Creator said
it was "not good" for Adam to be alone (Genesis 2:18).
Have you ever thought about this before? God created
Adam with a need that God himself could not meet.

Of course, God saw Adam's state before Adam
understood it. Instead of creating a companion the

moment he saw the need, God wanted Adam to discover his aloneness. I believe that is part of the reason God gave him the job of naming every animal on the planet.

Day after day, month after month, perhaps even year after year, Adam examined animal after animal, giving each a unique name. Early on, he surely noticed each animal had been created in pairs, male and female. We can only wonder whether this realization fueled a desperate quest for his unique companion. If so, he never found her. But he did learn he was uniquely alone.

That's when God stepped in. He caused Adam to fall into a deep sleep, extracted a rib from his side, and delicately sculpted his perfect match. God crafted each curve of her body—eyes, lips, hair, breasts, legs, feet, arms, and hands—to be just what Adam needed. And just what he desired.

> *Like liquid poured into a glass,*
> *she would empty his world*
> *of aloneness,*
> *and fill it with*
> *her love.*

When God had placed the final touch on his greatest masterpiece, he nudged her in Adam's direction and left as quietly as a cloud. Adam awoke, rubbed his eyes, climbed to his feet, and wandered through the garden, probably searching for another animal to name.

Suddenly, he stopped and stared. He had never seen the creature who stood before him. In a way, she looked like him. But she also looked different—beautifully different. After years alone, without a companion with whom to talk, laugh, dream, hold, and make love, Adam finally beheld his match—the crown of God's creation. She was flawless: physically,  mentally, spiritually. She possessed every attribute Adam could ever want in a lover and friend. And she carried no baggage from her past. No corrosive bitterness, ugly scars, crippling regrets, or selfish expectations (or belly button). She had no stain, she was without par.

In Genesis 2:23, we find Adam's response at this very moment.

> *"At last! ...*
> ***This one is bone from my bone,***
> ***and flesh from my flesh!"***
> *(New Living Translation)*

In all of creation, he had never seen beauty like hers. And it caused a romantic celebration the old-fashioned way—with poetic verse.

This helps explain why men are attracted to women. They are God's masterpiece, created to replace our aloneness with companionship.

If you're married, your search is over, like Adam's was once he met Eve. You've found your life partner, your best friend and lover.

Maybe, like last night's dream, you've forgotten this truth.[15] And having forgotten, you've returned to the search. You catch yourself gazing at a female co-worker or a woman passing on the street, wondering if she could provide the companionship your heart longs for. Not that you're unhappy with your wife. But maybe you are, maybe you don't feel what you felt in the past. Perhaps you enjoy the hunt, the pursuit of something you desire deep within.

Listening to Jesus often clears my mind. Every month over the past year, I've read through all four Gospels. One thing I've noticed is the importance Jesus placed on the marriage union. He didn't focus on past marital mistakes, but on present and future behavior. He said, "Therefore, what God has joined together, let no one separate" (Mark 10:9, NIV). If you're married, God wants your union to endure.[16] This truth relieves you of wondering if your wife will be your lifelong companion. Hopefully it will prompt you to hold fast to your marriage vows and thank God your search is over.

Remember, every woman offers the hope of replacing your aloneness with companionship. But God sent one woman to fill that role . . . your wife.

A WOMAN'S NEED FOR FRIENDSHIP

Because your wife was created to be your companion, it should be no surprise that *she needs you to be her best friend and closest confidant.* The one God brought into your life to resolve your aloneness needs to know she fills your heart in this way. Solomon put this principle into practice on the night of his wedding when he said:

> *This is my beloved,*
> *And this is my friend.*

(Song of Songs 5:16, American Standard Version)

While friendship within marriage is not the sexiest topic, studies indicate it is actually the most important factor in marital satisfaction. This point is emphasized in *Real Marriage*, a book by Seattle-based pastor, Mark Driscoll.[17] In his book, Driscoll cites a preeminent sociologist's study on marriage, which found, "The determining factor in whether wives feel satisfied with the sex, romance, and passion in their marriage is, by 70 percent, the quality of the couple's friendship. For men, the determining factor is, by 70 percent the quality of the couple's friendship. So men and women come from the same planet after all."[18] The study went on to conclude:

> Happy marriages are based on a deep friendship. By this I mean a mutual respect for and enjoyment of each other's company. These couples tend to know each other intimately—they are well versed in each other's likes, dislikes, personality quirks, hopes, and dreams. They have an abiding regard for each other and express this fondness not just in the big ways but in little ways day in and day out. . . . Friendship fuels the flames

for romance because it offers the best protection against feeling adversarial toward your spouse.[19]

It's important to catch that last point: friendship with your wife protects against adversarial bitterness— and infidelity—by *fueling the flames of romance*. So friendship isn't just a need within your wife, it's also a need within you.

DEEPEN YOUR FRIENDSHIP WITH YOUR WIFE

Maintaining a deep and fun friendship with your wife should be a top priority. Here are four practical ways to make it happen. Do them daily and you'll find yourself in a deeper, more fulfilling marriage.

➤ First, listen to your wife.

In 1 Peter 3:7, husbands are told to "live with your wife in an understanding way" (NASB). The only way a man can understand his wife is to listen to her. Ask her questions. Seek to discover her desires and passions, what worries and troubles her, what brings her happiness and joy.

It's important that you *understand* what she's saying rather than try to fix her problem. Women usually prefer an *ear* to a wrench. Make it your goal to understand

first. Only then should you concern yourself with being understood.

If you need to improve in this area, tell your wife you want to learn to listen better. Ask her for listening tips. Give her permission to let you know when she feels you're not paying attention. When she calls you out, don't defend yourself. Instead apologize and ask some leading questions. Your willingness to ask questions is critical because it shows you're not self-focused.

Avoid a harsh or sarcastic tone.[20] A gentle tone tells her you're sincere, that you value her companionship and are trying to deepen your friendship. It will show you're putting her needs before your own. Such love builds trust and forms the foundation for a lasting, lifelong friendship.

➤ Second, quickly reconcile differences.

Paul said, "Do not let the sun go down while you are still angry" (Ephesians 4:26, NIV). I don't think Paul meant we must resolve every conflict and defuse all anger literally before sunset. But I do think he identified a critical principle for married couples: when conflict arises, make peace quickly. Ideally, you'll do this often enough so that anger will never reach a destructive level. If your anger has reached that level, you should meet with a pastor or counselor.[21]

Early in our marriage, Cindy and I agreed to talk through any unprocessed anger before going to sleep.[22] We had some late nights but it taught us the importance of defusing anger before it expands and explodes, or settles and implodes. And it always drew us closer together than before the initial fracture. That is the miracle of reconciliation. This commitment protected our friendship and gave God a chance to heal any anger and bitterness.

I understand that sometimes making wise decisions in the heat of an argument can seem as difficult as orchestrating your dreams. That's why you and your wife must identify exercises that allow either of you to take a break and reduce the temperature. Taking a short break—a walk alone or time in Scripture, for example—to achieve perspective and allow intense emotions to rebalance may be helpful.

My son, Paul, noticed a pattern with his fiancé: when they're tired, they more easily spiral into arguments that by the next morning seem silly. So they have agreed not to broach controversial issues after 9:00 p.m. If one of them says something contentious and it's after the cutoff time, the other can immediately table the discussion *until the next day*. It's these sorts of simple solutions that allow couples to process anger or frustrations quickly and lovingly.

> ➤ Third, have fun together.

We all need a regular break from the mutual maintenance duties we perform every day. We need to go on regular dates and have fun. I suggest instituting a weekly date night—at the very least, make it a monthly occasion. If you have children, it's important to leave them at home or to have someone watch them. This is time for you and your wife to build your relationship.

A recent article in *The New York Times* noted the important connection between healthy marriages and the mutual enjoyment of "exciting" activities. It instructs couples to "eschew predictability in favor of discovery, novelty and opportunities for unpredictable pleasure."[23] Find a recreational activity you both like and enjoy it together. Seek out new hobbies or events that require both of you to step outside of your comfort zone.

> ➤ Fourth, thank God your search for a female companion is over.

Celebrate that God has brought you a lifetime lover and friend. And remember, *your wife needs you to be her best friend and closest companion, and she needs you to verbalize how much you love and appreciate her.*

Incorporate the above suggestions into your marriage and your marriage will deepen and the level of marital satisfaction will increase. If you're skeptical, try it for one month. These actions, and the attitudes behind them, are so powerful in sparking relational transformation that you will almost certainly adopt them into your everyday life.

As your friendship with your wife grows, you'll develop a deeper appreciation for the fourth reason naked women look so good.

Review

- ☐ **Why naked women look so good:** To replace aloneness with companionship.
- ☐ **What need this reveals in your wife:** She needs the two of you to be best friends.
- ☐ **How you should act:** Deepen your friendship with your wife by loving, listening to, forgiving, and having fun with her.

Chapter 4

WHOLENESS

The moment God brought Eve to Adam he received a much improved version of the rib he had lost. At their first meeting, Adam came face to face, chest to breasts, thighs to thighs, with the part of himself that was missing. What had been lost was found.

In light of the creation story, it makes sense that the beauty of a woman's body is mysteriously linked to a man's search for completeness. At the deepest level of his subconscious, there is a part of every man that craves his earliest father's missing rib, his one true Eve. Every man longs for the woman who will make him whole. He seeks the one whose absence he always feels.

I'm not saying a spouse will solve all of our problems or make us feel entirely complete. This is untrue and unbiblical—otherwise why would the Apostle Paul extol the virtues of singleness (1 Corinthians 7:7)? I'm speaking of relational completeness. For most of us, there is another person on this planet we hope will settle the restlessness in our hearts. They will be our other half . . . our completer.

The truth is, because we live in a fallen world, we will never feel entirely complete this side of heaven. We will always have a sense of unsettledness, a longing for *shalom*.[24] This is a holy hole. It is designed by God to be filled by God. As C. S. Lewis observed, "If I discover within myself a desire which no experience in this world can satisfy, the most probable explanation is that I was made for another world."[25]

Our wholeness will never be fully realized in this lifetime. Paul reminds us that believers groan within themselves as they await their adoption as sons (and daughters) and the redemption of their bodies (Romans 8:23). Our faith is built on a forward-looking hope. We ache to be reunited with our Creator. Paul stated our expectation beautifully when he wrote, "No eye has seen, no ear has heard, and no mind has imagined what God has prepared for those who love him" (1 Corinthians 2:9, NLT). If a man or woman thinks getting married will fill their internal ache, they will be bitterly disappointed. But a loving marriage can bring with it a powerful sense of relational wholeness.

Of course, singles can and do find fulfillment in life. After all, Jesus and the apostle Paul were single and their lives overflowed. The Bible makes it clear

that some people are gifted with singleness in order
to uniquely advance God's kingdom (Matthew 19:12).
But most singles, particularly those without this gift,
have learned to live with a steady, unsettled sense of
aloneness, a quiet awareness that they are alone, by
themselves, missing something or someone.

For men, that sense of emptiness creates a desire
to find their figurative missing rib. It propels every
man to discover the one person who will make him feel
relationally complete, like Eve did for Adam.[26] And for
every man, like the first one, God designed a woman to
meet this need. Because of this:

> *In the moment a man gazes*
> *at a woman's naked beauty,*
> *he experiences, for a fleeting second,*
> *the hope of being made whole.*

It makes sense that God would create man to feel
magnetically pulled to the one who has the presence
to fill the emptiness in his heart. And once he finds
her, with his rib snugly in place, he no longer needs to
search for someone to fill the gap in his soul because
it's gone.

I'll never forget the amazing sense of pleasure I
experienced after marriage. I'm not speaking of sex, but
of lying in bed with my arms wrapped around Cindy. I
felt a sense of contentment I had never imagined.

Most single guys don't spend time thinking about
cuddling with their future wife. Their thoughts are on
a more active embrace.

A WOMAN'S NEED FOR COMPLETENESS

I was no different. What I didn't anticipate was the overwhelming sense of completeness I felt just being with Cindy. But I wasn't alone in my joy. She too found contentment in me.

That last sentence is crucial because it indicates Cindy needed me as much as I needed her. Just as a man needs a women to complete him, *a woman needs a man to complete her.* Without a man, she feels alone. She wonders about her value and worth. She questions her loveliness and beauty.[27]

For a little girl, these important questions are answered—for better or for worse—by her father.[28] As she develops into a woman, she begins looking beyond her family of origin and listening to the messages, both implicit and explicit, conveyed by society, friends, boyfriends, media, and even God. With conflicting explanations and the shifting importance of relationships, this can be a time of deep insecurity and confusion not only for girls, but also for boys.

This is a normal period for adolescents and young adults in our culture and often involves dating, changes in social groups, and various forms of experimentation.

At its core, it is about determining who to believe in answering the big identity-defining life questions— who am I and does my life have value? Girls often spend this time looking for that special man who will unconditionally love and appreciate her. A man who will help her blossom so she can fulfill her God-given purpose.

When a woman gets married, her husband is supposed to fill this role. Other than God, a husband should be the primary figure who answers a woman's important life questions about value and worth and loveliness. And while men surely want their wife to answer these questions with confidence—*I am of utmost value, worth, and loveliness*—most guys have no idea how they fit into this process. Some think this issue should have been resolved on their wedding day or that expressing their love is an annual requirement met with a Hallmark card on Valentine's Day. Of course, *women need their husband to play a continuing, active role in ensuring their internal sense of completeness.*

VALIDATE YOUR WIFE

Think about this: even in a strong and healthy marriage, women can feel incomplete—unsure about their value, worth, and loveliness—and can struggle with personal discontentment. Your responsibility as a husband isn't to argue with your wife about how she feels, but to share how she makes *you* feel. In order to feel complete, your wife needs to know how she affects you, how she completes you, how she makes your life more fulfilling. And you need to *repeatedly* tell her, even when you think she's already heard it.

Here's the challenge I suggest trying for a week:

> ➤ Take some time and think about how your wife completes you. Once you've identified several ways, tell her daily how she makes you a better man.

Before sitting down to draft this chapter, I talked with Cindy about some initial concepts. During the course of the conversation, Cindy asked a question that clarified the importance of a husband's role in defining his wife's sense of completeness. She asked, "What have I accomplished with my life?"

"To begin with," I said, "God has used you to transform me. What would I be without you? You're the ballast that keeps me upright. You're strong where I'm weak. I was a swamp and you turned me into a river. What have you accomplished? You've been the person God used, more than any other, to change my life."

"Really?" she asked. "Do you really feel that way?"

38

"I really feel that way," I said as I took her into my arms.

We crave that moment of completeness when our souls are at rest in the arms of the woman we love. And she seeks a man who will complete her.

Review

- ❏ **Why naked women look so good:** They offer the hope of wholeness.
- ❏ **What need this reveals in your wife:** She needs you to complete her.
- ❏ **What you should do:** Validate how your wife completes you.

Chapter 5

HER GLORY

In his book *The Mystery of Marriage*, Mike Mason notes that the human body "possesses a glory that is unique in all the earth."[29] By glory he meant "awe-inspiring beauty." In a sense, our bodies reveal who we are. They are the physical expression of our soul and spirit. The body of a woman is more than skin and bones, eyes and hair. It is the veil of her person.

Several times in the Old Testament, God revealed himself with a physical manifestation. We refer to these manifestations as the glory of God. And the glory of God speaks of the beauty and power that emanates from his character, from all he is within.

The psalmist wrote, "The heavens declare the glory of God" (Psalm 19:1, NIV). As countless stars, planets, and moons silently glide overhead, they remind every eye of the God who placed them there.

Elsewhere the psalmist wrote, "The God of glory thunders" (Psalm 29:3, NIV). God's glory engages not only the eyes, but the ears. Rolling thunder leaps from the sky, it tumbles through forests, summersaults down hills, and bounds over lakes. It claps, silencing animals and startling men. The thundering voice of God speaks with power.

Such revelations of God's glory are for all to see and hear. But on occasion, God gives a special glimpse of his glory. He did that when he appeared to Moses on the mountain as a fire in a bush. Later, he appeared to Moses and the Israelites on Mount Sinai as a thick cloud filled with lightning. The glory of God hung densely at Mount Sinai—so much so that when Moses left the Lord's presence, his face glowed.

God created a woman's body to display a glory of its own, a glory that reveals not only the brilliance of the God who created her, but also the beauty of her soul. Her cheeks, eyes, hair, and shoulders are not simply beautiful to gaze upon, they are the windows through which we come to know the precious person within. The loveliness of her breasts, waist, hips, and legs are not just a wonder to behold; they promise a deeper, inner beauty that we long to discover.

To be sure, a woman's beauty exceeds that of a night sky, autumn leaves, crashing waves, or a setting sun. She is the

pinnacle of God's creation. But like every manifestation of God's glory, its source is far greater. A woman is deeper than her physical frame, more magnificent than mere flesh and blood. Her body radiates the soul and spirit of a living person filled with hopes and dreams, fears and disappointments. And like Moses on the mountain, we yearn not only to glimpse her glory, but to experience it.

I agree with Charles Spurgeon who said the second greatest request ever made by a man occurred when Moses asked God to teach him his ways so he could know him and find his favor (Exodus 33:13, NIV).[30] While dating, this is what a man does with a woman. He listens with the skill of a counselor, trying to discover her heart so he can capture her love. He applies all he has learned so he can tell her what she needs to hear and give her what she needs to receive.

Moses asked a great question. But he made a greater request a few verses later. After God told Moses he was pleased with him, the lawgiver boldly said, "Now show me your glory" (Exodus 33:18, NIV).

Once a man knows a woman and has won her trust in marriage, he asks to see what she holds sacred.

A WOMAN'S NEED TO BE UNDERSTOOD

This desire to see and enter a woman's glory has great appeal and gives another reason why naked women look so good. But it also reveals that a *woman needs the man in her life to understand her not just during courtship, but throughout marriage. She needs to know you love the person within, not simply the beauty of her body.* You don't accomplish this overnight, but by showing interest over time.

Because your wife's thoughts and feelings are changing just as yours are, it's crucial you continually seek to know her. Study her. Ask her questions. Learn new things about her. In this way, you'll know her better and deepen your love. In the process, she'll learn that your love for her is holistic, not simply physical.

One important aspect of loving your wife from within is showing her respect physically. What I mean is, a woman needs to invite a man into her glory. Sexual intimacy is *always* a mutual act. A man must never force himself on a woman, even his wife. Her spirit and body must be open for him to draw near. Before he enters her beauty, she must give him permission, verbally or physically. A man should always respect the feelings and needs of his wife, even above his own (1 Corinthians 7:4).

Your wife must know you view her body as sacred and will always treat her with respect. Such knowledge liberates her to love without fear.

Another critical element to understanding your wife and helping her feel understood is praising the source of her glory—her soul and spirit—not exclusively her physical beauty.

I once asked Cindy if she ever got tired of me praising her. Faster than a blink she said, "No, not at all. Do it more!"

While I regularly celebrate her beauty, I also want her to know I love the person her glory reveals. There are few things you could do to build up your wife more than praising her physical beauty. But you must also praise her character. This is crucial because like autumn leaves her skin will slowly wilt over time. If she thinks you only love her body, she will question your love and age sorrowfully. But if she knows you love *her person*, she will age joyfully.

> **You need to know your wife so well**
> **you can sincerely praise her innermost person.**

I frequently tell Cindy how much I appreciate her amazing faith in God, her emotional stability, her attention to detail, her sense of humor. Really, the list could go on and on and sometimes it does.

I love praising my wife because I see the empowering effect on her face. Words of praise fill her love bank, making it easier for her to love me.

The glory of your wife's nakedness releases tremendous power inside of you. Rely upon it not only to praise the wonder of her body, but to praise the beauty of her inner person.

UNDERSTAND YOUR WIFE AND PRAISE HER

I challenge you, over a two-week period, to focus on better understanding your wife by asking her a thoughtful and caring question at least once a day. This will not only help you come to know your wife at a deeper level, but it will also show her that you're interested in her inner self. This affirmation will show her that you care and it will have far-reaching effects, from improving her self-image to growing her love for you. Here are a few questions that will get you started.[31]

- "How are you feeling today?" If she answers that she's feeling "fine" or "okay," ask for more details. "How is your heart?" or "How do you feel inside?" are good follow-ups.
- "What has God has been teaching you recently?"
- "What are you looking forward to these days?"
- "If you could ask God for anything, what would it be?"
- "What was the best and worst part of your day/week/month/year?"

I also challenge you to take this time to praise your wife's character and beauty throughout the day. As you do so, be sure and notice the empowering effect of your words. This is a practice you'll want to continue beyond two weeks.

If you're not sure what to say, here are some suggestions. From there, you might be inspired to create your own personalized list:

- "You're beautiful."
- "I'm glad I get to share my life with you."
- "You have gorgeous eyes."
- "I trust you."
- "I love to kiss your lips."
- "I thank God for your character."
- "Your kisses taste sweet to me."
- "You're such a blessing to me."
- "I love to look at and caress your legs."
- "You're a godly woman."
- "I can't wait to touch you all over."
- "I truly respect you."
- "I can't wait to feel your body against mine."

Just the other day I read this list to Cindy to see how she would respond. I expected her to laugh it off since I was, after all, reading a list. Instead, she beamed.

After you've praised your wife, take another step and repeatedly thank God for the wonder of her glory . . . a glory you have the privilege to see and enter. As you praise your wife for her beauty, she'll become more beautiful in your eyes and in her own.

Review

- ❑ **Why naked women look so good:** Their glory reveals soul and spirit.
- ❑ **What need this reveals in your wife:** She needs you to continually seek to understand her.
- ❑ **What you should do:** Ask your wife questions and praise her character and beauty.

INTIMACY

When a woman amorously removes her clothes for a man, he thinks she's inviting him to make love.[32] In a guy's world, nakedness presupposes sexual intimacy. For a woman, undressing before a man is not simply about sex, but relational intimacy. In fact, God designed sexual intimacy to presuppose relational intimacy.

It should go without saying that prior to disrobing before a man, a woman must first trust him. Or at least want to trust him. As her clothes fall away, a woman relinquishes much power, uncovering both beauty and blemish. When she's clothed, he cannot see her defects, real or invented. By revealing her body, though, a woman exposes everything—not just her skin, but also her heart—and in doing so, surrenders to a man the power to accept or reject her. Her deepest longing is for him to marvel at her nakedness and celebrate her body, despite its imperfections.

While all women are aware of their physical flaws, today's culture idolizes female beauty, creating an environment ripe for women to feel insecure about their own appearance. The media showcases only the most ideal figures of beauty—young women at the zenith of their glory. The average size of the "ideal" woman, as portrayed by models, has become progressively thinner over the years, stabilizing at around 20 percent below the average weight. This standard is unachievable for most women. One study found that three minutes spent looking at models in a fashion magazine caused 70 percent of women to feel depressed, guilty, and ashamed.[33]

It is an unrealistically high standard for women to measure up against, nudged even higher by technology that literally  erases every imperfection, trace of cellulite, blemish, and wrinkle in these images. The most beautiful women are further perfected, sculpted into modern-day demigods. At the same time, our culture conveniently ignores the temporal nature of beauty which fades like a rainbow.

It's important for men to understand that when women, in the privacy of their bathrooms, look at themselves in the mirror, they compare their bodies—every line and curve—to this impossible ideal. Or they privately undress in a room with no mirrors. Your wife walks into the bedroom with the cards stacked against her. She undresses before you with great vulnerability.

I'm reminded of a recent article about Britney Spears, once the most worshiped teenage pop star, in which along with an advertisement flaunting her still-perfect body, she publicly released the original, unedited version of the same picture used in the ad.[34] Side by side, the two photos look like they are of women with different bodies. One is ideal, the other is *real*.

The point is, when a woman undresses before a man, she is revealing her body. But on a deeper level, she is exposing her soul. She is hoping the one man she loves will tell her she is beautiful, despite the flaws and imperfections. This is the longing of every woman: to give a man her body *and* her soul.

Adam and Eve possessed intimacy untainted by sin and imperfection. They had no standard by which to judge and condemn one another. After God brought them together, we read, "The man and his wife were both naked and were not ashamed" (Genesis 2:25, NASB).

They felt no shame about their bodies, their personalities, or their personal histories. Their physical nakedness portrayed the nakedness that existed at a spiritual and emotional level. Adam and Eve were intimate in every sense of the word.

Since that first meeting of a naked man and women, much damage has been done to the male psyche. While men avoid intimacy, they desperately need it. But our culture and upbringing have programmed most guys to believe *real* men are rugged, self-sufficient, and independent. While I realize the idea of men being tough on the outside isn't as prevalent as it was in the past, men still crave independence. However, this strong need for independence doesn't override his craving for an intimate link with a woman.

Singer Kenny Chesney captured the idea with his song, "You Had Me from Hello." The lyrics describe a man who felt confident he would never be hurt because he built a strong wall around his heart. But that wall proved no match for the touch of a woman. And so he sings,

"Bricks of my defenses scattered on the ground."[35]

While we grit our teeth and go it alone, we long for a woman we can know inside and out, a woman who will see us as the man of her dreams, her shining prince.

We long for a woman whose touch will knock down the bricks of our defenses, scattering them on the ground.

Naked women are beautiful because their nakedness says, "You're the greatest man I know. I offer you my body and my inner self."

That message connects with a man because it means she has chosen him above all others. He is the one she's been waiting for. The one who will rescue her. Such affirmation speaks to a man's deepest emotional needs.

*God made naked women appealing to men
by wiring men in such a way
that they view nakedness as an offer of intimacy.*

There is a danger, though. Men, for example, who peer at naked women through the window of the Internet taste this intimacy. In a hidden place they satisfy their every fantasy. But it's an illusion. It's food that cannot fill. The same applies to men who visit nudie bars, look at salacious magazines, or daydream about their coworker or neighbor.

Such men are forever discontent, endlessly searching for the perfect female body. Their search prevents them from finding true intimacy with a woman. Why? Because they are unable to accept as beautiful the imperfect body of a real woman—and *every* real woman has flaws. Only a woman fully accepted can feel loved. And only a loved woman will find the safety needed to open her soul to a man.

Because nakedness communicates intimacy, women who publicly exhibit their bodies exercise great power over men. But any connection momentarily experienced is superficial. It's an illusion of intimacy that will leave him worse off than before. While he may be sexually relieved for a short while, he will be left with a deep yearning for more—like an addict who needs an increasing amount of his favorite drug to get the same rush.

What starts as a glance on the Internet leads to untold hours of browsing the Web, scouring thousands of images. It can escalate to video chat rooms and animalistic[36] sexual experiences that further harden a man's heart, leaving him unable to know true intimacy. He is a parched man, lost in a desert, trying to fill a punctured canteen with a mirage.

Tragically, a man's obsession with porn or other women, real or fantastical, rejects the trust his wife offered the first time she undressed for him. At the deepest level, she hoped and prayed he would love her and be enthralled  with her beauty. She feared his rejection but he assured her of his love.

Now he has betrayed her trust and hides part of himself from her. He lives a shadowed existence, slipping in and out of a life she knows nothing about. He can minimize the secret and convince himself it's no big deal. Or he can justify his actions by telling himself he has needs she can't or won't meet.

In the end he's divided. The ideal—the mirage— offers no intimacy. If he chooses it, he will not only end up isolated from his wife. It will be much worse. He will end up alone.

WOMEN NEED EMOTIONAL INTIMACY

This places two options before a man. He can choose real intimacy with his wife, or he can choose counterfeit intimacy with an image or another woman. The first option is based on open and honest communication that builds trust and produces ever-expanding intimacy. The second is based on deceit and leads to isolation.[37]

Intimacy requires trust because trust creates safety. A woman only exposes her vulnerable places to a man she trusts won't betray her . . . a faithful man who celebrates her beauty alone.

As a woman, she needs to know you at the deepest level. From personal experience and the experiences of countless couples, nothing facilitates such knowledge more than praying together. That's why I urge you to pray with your wife in the morning or at night. It doesn't have to be a long or particularly religious prayer. Just talk with God. Thank him for the ways he has shown you his goodness. Pray for your wife and family. Pray for any special needs you share.

Last year I received an e-mail from a man who took my advice and prayed with his wife, for the first time, while they were in bed one night. He said he had prayed with their children many times as he tucked them in bed. But he had never prayed with his wife. She was so moved by his prayer that tears ran down her cheeks. By opening this essential channel, they reached a level of intimacy they had never shared before.

I don't know how your wife will respond, but I believe your prayers will draw you closer to the Lord and each other. As God answers your prayers, your faith will grow and so will the love you and your wife have for each other.

True intimacy—intimacy that is both reciprocal and fulfilling—can only occur in a safe setting, in an environment where a woman's nakedness is an expression of her soul's need to know and be known. When a man understands this and seeks to find in her nakedness not only sexual pleasure but an intimate connection, he will build a marriage that will last a lifetime. A marriage defined by open, honest, and loving communication with each other and God.

The soul of every man hungers for female intimacy. He wants a woman to see him completely and love him still. He wants to be her hero, champion, prince, and rescuer. This need for intimacy adds to the beauty and appeal of a woman's body. And it's the sixth reason why naked women look so good.

PRAY WITH YOUR WIFE

Several years ago I conducted an Internet survey among Christian men of different ages and from different parts of the United States. I was interested in finding out how often they prayed with their wife. Almost 60 percent of the respondents indicated they seldom or never prayed with their wife. If you fit into that category, you're not alone. Yet praying with your wife strengthens intimacy more than anything else.

With that in mind, your challenge is to take a few minutes each day for one week and pray with your wife. If you're already praying with her, keep it up.

While you may initially feel uncomfortable, take the leap. Tell her you would like to pray for her and your family. And then talk to God in a casual conversational way. You might say something like this,

> *Father, thank you for this day (mention a few things you're thankful for). I pray you'll give—your wife's name—physical and emotional strength for (pray for a specific need in her life). I thank you for her (mention something specific about your wife that you're thankful for). I pray for my family (pray for your kids or other family members by name). I pray you'll meet our need for (mention a need the two of you have). I pray you'll give us a great night's sleep (or a great day if you pray in the morning). In Christ's name, amen.*

Even if praying with your wife feels awkward, give it a try. It won't take long for you to feel as comfortable praying as you do talking with a friend. And it won't take long for your conversations with God to open the way to your wife's heart.

Review

- ☐ **Why naked women look so good:** They give the hope of intimacy.
- ☐ **What need this reveals in your wife:** She needs to have an intimate relationship with you.
- ☐ **What you should do:** Pray with your wife.

Chapter 7

A SEXUAL PLAYMATE

September in Austin is hot. Not as hot as Phoenix, but more humid and sticky. One afternoon while Cindy and I tried to hide from the heat in our matchbox-sized apartment on Cedar Street, near the University of Texas campus, the phone rang. It was one of those black plastic boxes with a dialer like a clock and holes over the numbers. I picked up the receiver.

"Hello," I said.

"Hi," the caller said with a sweet southern drawl. "This is Diane Dawson. We met at a party at Joe Glickman's house in Dallas last year. I told you I'd call when I came to Austin. Well, I'm here and hoped we could get together."

Tall and slender with dark hair and

a nice figure, I remembered Diane. "I'm flattered you called, but I got married last month."

"Oh," she responded, her voice deflated. "I guess that means you're not available." She paused for a moment. "Right?"

I sensed from her tone that she thought after four weeks of marriage, I might be ready for a break. "Yeah, that's right," I said. "But thanks for calling."

As soon as I hung up, I was confronted with the profound reality that for the rest of my life, I would never date, kiss, cuddle with, or have sex with a woman besides my wife.

I swallowed hard.

"Who was that?" Cindy asked.

"Diane Dawson."

"Who?"

"A girl I met at Joe's."

"What did she want?"

"To hang out."

"Hang out?"

"Right. But I told her I was in love with the most beautiful sexy woman alive, who happens to be my wife."

"I didn't hear you say that."

"Well, maybe I didn't. But it's true."

Cindy smiled, wrapped her arms around me, and squeezed tight.

That experience reminds me that one reason men marry is because they want a lover to hold . . . a playmate to frolic with. A lot of guys think God frowns on such desires. They believe since the Bible extols sexual purity, God views sex grudgingly and only approves of one sexual activity and position—and then only for procreation.

It can be hard to convince this type of guy that God not only designed sex to be enjoyed, but that he *celebrates* sex. He may reject such an idea because of a destructive upbringing or he associates sex with past sinful behaviors or current struggles. His history fills a backpack

with sexual memories he drags into bed and rummages through while making love to his wife. He knows God disapproves of "impure" thoughts and so he reasons God must be unhappy with him, even while having sex with his wife.

Saying the words, "God celebrates sex," feels awkward to guys like this. Yet embracing God's view of sex has a liberating power. How much more would a man enjoy making love with his wife if he knew God blessed their every action, from foreplay to climax?

The truth is, God wired men (and women) to desire physical intimacy and enjoy sex. And he created marriage as the ideal playground. Men and women who marry don't simply exchange vows. They also commit to pursue sexual intimacy together.

From God's perspective, marriage is the only place a man can fully enjoy a woman's body. Granted, as we saw in the last chapter, some men choose to find sexual pleasure outside of marriage, through either real or fantasy-based affairs. But each sexual partner dilutes his soul, preventing him from finding the intimacy that pleases God and nurtures his soul. It's in the context of marriage that sexual pleasure may be fully embraced and heartily enjoyed. It's in this setting that commitment and creativity play a crucial role in a healthy sex life.

Let's examine what the Bible actually says about God's view of sex.

Tucked away in the middle of the Old Testament is the poetic book, Song of Songs. The book describes the rapturous love between Solomon and his bride. The language is so graphic that for years theologians insisted the book be interpreted allegorically. By allowing Solomon to represent Christ, and his young bride the church, they avoided having to confront the explicit imagery. But such an interpretation doesn't do justice to either the text or to God.

In his book *A Song for Lovers*, my friend S. Craig Glickman said of the couple, "Their love is consummated in one of the shyest and most delicate of love scenes in world literature."[38] Solomon's writing is delicate and poetic, a breathtaking expression of romantic love. Though he speaks vividly of intimacy, there is nothing crude in his speech. He tenderly refers to his bride as a garden and fountain (verses 12–15). He makes a gentle allusion to her virginity by observing that her fountain is sealed and her garden locked (verse 12). No one before has entered. Finally the night for a visitor has arrived.

Solomon declares her fountain has become a "well of flowing water" (verse 15). Aroused by his expressions of delight, she pleads with him to "come into her garden and taste its choice fruits" (verse 16). Before doing so, he finds himself swept away by her beauty, describing her garden as a paradise of fruits, flowers, blossoms, trees, and aromatic spices.[39] There is no mistaking the meaning of these words.

Prior to lowering the shades on his honeymoon suite, Solomon leaves us with a final, climactic declaration. Amazingly, the words are not spoken by Solomon or his bride. They are uttered by God. He says to them,

> *"Eat, O friends, and drink;*
> *drink your fill, O lovers"*
> *(Song of Songs 5:1).*

As with Solomon on his wedding night, today God encourages—and *blesses*—sexual intimacy between husband and wife. Not simply on the night of the wedding, but throughout marriage. Indeed, married couples are encouraged to "drink their fill"—to enjoy sex as often as desired. The New Testament in 1 Corinthians 7:5 affirms this teaching, providing that the only reason a couple should mutually refrain from sex is for a season of focused prayer.

Naked women look good to men because it is while naked they engage in sexual play. Amazingly, a woman's body is both the playground and playmate. And when couples play, God celebrates.

WOMEN NEED YOU TO MOVE AT THEIR PACE

I'll never forget teaching my youngest son, Paul, how to drive my shiny black, showroom new, very fast Dodge Viper. Actually, it was a five-speed Mazda—gutless—Miata. Teaching him the timing between easing the clutch and accelerating the gas was as fun as a wooden carnival ride. I had forgotten how jer . . . jer . . . jerky a ride could be when the driver hadn't yet learned to operate a manual transmission.

I also had forgotten the difficulty a new driver has sensing *when* to shift gears. Initially, Paul would shift from first to second to third before the engine had enough RPMs to propel the car forward. One afternoon, as he drove up Overlook Drive, a half-mile-long, 20 percent 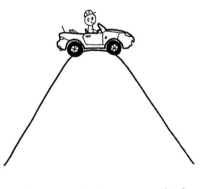 grade hill near our home, the car rolled to a stop before reaching the summit. Paul now faced the additional challenge of coordinating the gas and clutch while the car rolled downhill . . . backwards.

And I faced the challenge of not freaking out—the joys of fatherhood.

Of course, it didn't take long for him to get the timing down. Now he drives a black five-speed Hyundai Elantra with ease and grace.[40]

Unfortunately, a lot of men never achieve that same level of success with their wives. Many men try to shift from first gear to fifth before their wife has built up enough sexual energy to reach the summit. This is an all-too common problem with men that reveals the differences in how men and women were designed. After several minutes, most men's sexual tachometer is redlining and they're ready to shift gears. Women are different. Just as the man is redlining, she's reaching 1,000 RPMs.

One afternoon while Cindy and I had the house to ourselves, she began to slowly caress my shoulders, back, neck, head, arms, and hands. When she had caressed all of those body parts, she returned to my shoulders, and then continued on to my back, neck, arms, and hands. She repeated this cycle two more times.

When I asked why she wasn't progressing along, she told me she wasn't ready. The truth is, she was moving along as quickly as she could. Since her engine was only hitting 1,000 RPMs, she needed me to move slowly and not shift gears until she was close to the redline.

A woman needs you to move at her sexual pace. *If you want to meet your wife's sexual needs, stay in first gear until you sense she's ready to shift.* And to make it even more fun for her, wait until her RPMs are redlining.

The key is to move slowly. Give her time to warm up and even boil over.

SEEK YOUR WIFE'S GRATIFICATION FIRST

Of course, all of this would be much easier if you knew what she liked. Don't make the mistake of assuming she likes something just because you've done it a thousand times. Discover what arouses her. Learn exactly where and how she likes to be touched. And find out how fast she wants you to move along.[41]

Here's how you learn:

- Since your wife is both the playground and playmate, devote an evening to giving her pleasure. Tell her you're going to follow her instructions. Let her tell you when to touch her, and where, and for how long. Select an evening when you won't be disturbed. Every caress and movement will be at the pace and place of her selection. If possible, take mental notes.

As your lovemaking progresses, remember: you're seeking her pleasure, not yours. Which for most men, not so coincidentally, occurs by watching their wife get aroused. So the more a husband pleases his wife, the more pleasure he experiences.

Review

- ❏ **Why naked women look so good:** They provide the potential for a sexual playmate
- ❏ **What need this reveals in your wife:** She needs you to meet her sexual needs at her pace.
- ❏ **What you should do:** Learn what pleases your wife and seek her gratification above your own.

A BRIDLE

God designed sex to be among the most meaningful and pleasurable experiences in all of life. In the joining of a man and a woman, they become "one flesh." During those exhilarating moments, the two are made whole. Their bodies are not simply linked physically, but spiritually and emotionally. It is the most intimate connection two people can share. No wonder God calls their union, "one flesh" (Genesis 2:24).

From the beginning, the Lord intended this oneness to occur within the safety of marriage. God's ideal has always been for a man to remain with a woman for a lifetime (Genesis 1:24). Unfortunately, the brokenness of humanity sometimes shatters this ideal and marriages end in divorce. Yet even when this happens, God's mercy can heal so the next marriage becomes the place of devotion.

While God made naked women beautiful to men, he wants a man to enjoy the nakedness of only one woman—*his wife*. You see, God created the marriage bed to provide a way to both satisfy and control the sexual appetite of both men and women.

If not controlled, our sexual desires have the potential to drive us to sin's doorstep. No man should forget that he corrals a ravenous beast with an insatiable appetite. That beast may occasionally sleep, but it will never lose the  ability to run wild, ravaging those we love.

Growing up in New Mexico, our family owned quarter horses that we kept outside of town. One summer morning, my dad drove me in his pickup to our property. Once there he taught me to use a saddle and bridle. Over the course of the summer, staying on the saddle got easier as my legs grew stronger. Learning to use a bridle took more time, though, because it required putting a bit into the horse's mouth while developing a sensitive touch when using it. Yet even as a boy, I could see the importance of a bridle. It enabled me, an 80 pound boy, to control a 1,500 pound animal.

While getting married is easy, a healthy marriage that incorporates what you've learned in this book is hard work. Part of that work involves keeping a tight rein on your sexual appetite.

For most guys, the idea of marriage serving as a sexual bridle only makes sense if their wife is physically attractive. According to Shaunti Feldhahn in her book, *For Women Only*, men place great importance upon their wife's appearance. But this isn't the whole story. Sexual attraction is not *solely* dependent on the physical appearance of a man's wife. Feldhahn gathered data from surveys and interviews that showed men are happy when they *see their wife make an effort to look her best.*[42]

Unfortunately, trying to look better can easily get out of hand.

Several years ago, I met a friend, Jason, at a coffee shop. A good-looking guy, Jason took pride in his workout routine and fast-track career. I could tell he was troubled and asked what was bothering him.

"I don't find my wife attractive anymore," he said.

"She's a beautiful woman," I said. "Maybe you should see an optometrist,"

Jason chuckled. "That's not it. She just doesn't turn me on like she used to."

"Why?" I asked.

He looked at the table and shook his head from side to side. "Well, ever since the birth of our son, her breasts sag." Glancing up, his eyes focused on me. "I want her to get a boob job. Not a big one. You know, maybe a D cup."

"Look," I said. "It's just a matter of time before both your bodies begin to sag. If you step on the treadmill of plastic surgery, she'll end up with a series of face-lifts, tummy-tucks, breast implants, and liposuctions."

"Funny you should mention that. We were thinking about going ahead with a tummy tuck while she's on the table. You know— tighten up the loose skin."

"Jason," I said. "You're not getting it."

"What do you mean?" he asked.

I thought for a moment, realizing Jason was blind to a key truth. Then I told him,

> *"The attraction between two magnets*
> *isn't based on their external appearance,*
> *but on their internal makeup.*
> *It's the same with love.*
> *Sustainable attraction*
> *between a man and a woman*
> *is based on what's inside."*

Jason didn't care. His wife got implants, but even they weren't perfect. He complained they didn't feel right.[43]

It's easy for a man to distance himself from his wife if he's unhappy with her  appearance and sees her make no effort to look better. Yet the spiritual implications are serious. If a man disregards his wife for any reason, he is disregarding God. Peter said as much when he wrote, "You husbands in the same way, live with your wives in an

72

understanding way, as with someone weaker, since she is a woman; and show her honor as a fellow heir of the grace of life, so that your prayers will not be hindered" (1 Peter 3:7, NASB).[44]

A man cannot ignore his wife and remain close to God. In fact, when we treat our wife with disrespect, it's a sure sign we've cut the anchor line and drifted from God.

Once a man strays from God and his wife, the marital vows he publicly affirmed lose their power. Instead of allowing them to bridle his passions, he drops the reins, letting his passions run wild. He no longer treats his wife as a companion who completes him and provides intimacy. He stops thinking of her as his one and only God-given sexual playmate, or as God's masterpiece whose body is a wonder and the glory of her person.

After a man disregards his vows, marriage is no longer a playground, but a prison. Locked in a relationship that no longer satisfies, the husband sees his wife as an obstacle to his pleasure, his happiness, and ultimately his life. He feels he must change her so she can meet his needs. If he believes she can't meet his needs, he may seek another woman who will meet them.

Such thinking stirs up emotional turmoil for a man because he realizes his actions would offend God and hurt those he loves most. He knows he would be placing a bomb beside someone who trusts him. Worse than that, he would detonate it. While an affair offers passionate sex, at least for a while, it will scar the innocence of his union, destroy trust, and deposit in his soul the venom of regret.[45]

Considering the high price to be paid for gratifying such longings, it's no surprise God commands us to focus our energy—sexual and emotional—on satisfying our wife, not ourselves. As men, we must remember that our body is for our wife. Our eyes are to look upon and enjoy her beauty alone (1 Corinthians 7:3-5). While we will notice beautiful women, we must guard our eyes and hearts from crossing the line between appreciating and greedily desiring.

That's the ideal we must strive for. Then and only then, within the arms of our wife, will we experience the kind of intimacy and pleasure God intends us to find in marriage.

A WOMAN'S NEED FOR SECURITY

Men often ask how they can enjoy their wife if her beauty has faded. I remind them of the words Solomon wrote concerning the wife of his youth. In Proverbs 5:18-19, he said:

> *"Rejoice in the wife of your youth.*
> *As a loving hind and a graceful doe,*
> *Let her breasts satisfy you at all times;*
> *Be exhilarated always with her love."*
> (NASB).

The imagery is of a man playing with his wife's breasts as he would a small deer (or in today's imagery, a puppy). But there are two key phrases that address the struggle many men face. Solomon's exhortation is to be practiced *always, at all times.* There is no exit clause—no age-expiration or weight-limit.

Even when a woman ages or becomes ill, the Bible commands men to "rejoice in the wife of your youth." While this doesn't give men permission to fantasize about the body of another woman, it does allow them to remember and celebrate the youthful body of their wife, even as she grows old.

If your wife is young, enjoy her beauty. Study her. Memorize every line. Know every curve. Imagine her throughout the day. Fill a mental vault with memories you can enjoy for a lifetime. Then love her with the same passion as long as you live. Because the most powerful sexual organ is the mind, use your imagination to recall your wife's beauty throughout the day. If your wife's beauty is fading, recall her former beauty. Make her, not another woman, the object of your fantasies. Allow her nakedness to intoxicate you.

It's possible you're thinking, *my wife is young but physically unattractive,* or *she's old and out of shape.* If you focus on her physical flaws, you'll do harm to both of you. Instead, rivet your eyes on the beauty she has, not the beauty she lacks.

Such focus stimulates love and sexual intimacy. It places a bridle in the hands of a man so he can control and direct his passions. But it accomplishes something else that's important to keep in mind. Namely, not only does the focused attention of a man help bridle his sexual passions, *it also meets the wife's need for relational security and increases her desire for sexual intimacy.*

Research tells us that married men,
who care for their wife,
meeting her need for love and security,
report having sex twice as frequently
as surveyed single men.[46]

CREATIVELY COMMUNICATE COMMITMENT WITH YOUR WIFE

The first exercise that will enable you to bridle your sexual energy involves controlling your thoughts toward other women. As I noted before, it's normal for you to be sexually attracted to other women. God wired you that way. But you must tap into God's grace and exercise discipline.

- The next time you see a woman and find sexual desire gaining a foothold, tell yourself, "I'm glad God created beautiful women and gave me the ability to appreciate them. But I belong to my wife." After saying this, imagine your wife's body at the height of her glory.

The second exercise involves creatively communicating commitment to your wife.

- Plan an evening alone with your wife. Take a bubble bath together—you'll need to buy the bubbly soap in advance. Afterward, give her a massage; begin with her feet and work your way up to her head. Move at her speed and direction. As you massage her, remind her of your commitment to her and assure her you only have eyes for her.[47]

It's important to always recognize that you wife is amazing. And her naked body is a wonder. Allow the energy generated by her beauty to empower you to love her in a way that meets her deepest needs. You will find that as her needs are met first, yours will be too.

Review

- ❏ **Why naked women look so good:** Her beauty has the ability to bring a man's passions under control.

- ❏ **What need this reveals in your wife:** Your wife needs relational security and sexual intimacy.

- ❏ **What you should do:** Communicate your commitment to your wife and bring creativity to the bedroom.

Chapter 9

LESSONS FROM A CHARIOT

One night while standing on the edge of an emotional vortex that threatened to pull me into a depression, I had a dream. This dream was so real and its message so life-giving that I've used it to help others overcome dark thoughts and feelings. In this chapter, I'll share my dream[i] and a spiritual exercise that will deliver you from deception and strengthen your love for your wife.

My Dream

It's spring. The sun softly touches my face. The cool air ruffles my hair and whisks away the sun's warmth. A field of green grass delights my eyes.

I'm in a chariot pulled by two horses, a black one on the left and a white one on the right. This is unlike riding horses as a boy. For one thing, I'm standing not sitting. And I've got two horses to manage, not one.

As they trot, their bodies bobbing up and down, the ride is smoother than expected. The fragrance of grass reminds me of fresh cut alfalfa.

The black horse suddenly darts to the left. I tug hard on the reins, trying to restrain him. The bit presses against the back of his mouth, jamming into his lips. It has no effect. I'm only a nuisance, a fly on his face. I've lost control.

He's running wild, ears back, eyes glazed, nostrils flared, pulling the other horse and chariot.

We're nearing the edge of the field, racing toward a thick stand of birch trees. I yell into the wind but the horse's hooves pound my words into silence.

The trees are advancing too quickly. There's nowhere to escape, no room to squeeze between the executioner's wooden blades.

THE BLACK HORSE

Awakening, I immediately knew the chariot represented my life and the black horse a mysterious propensity that battles against my "true" self (by true self, I mean who I am in Christ). You see, for much of my life I've felt unable to rein in the black horse. Where he ran, I followed. When he darted toward  danger, he dragged me along.

Of course, we've all ridden in a chariot pulled by a run-away horse. We know how it feels to be linked to his every twist and turn. Every man fights the beast within. Like a headless driver, we mindlessly follow where he pulls.

Fortunately, we aren't helplessly tied to the black horse. We can, and *must,* control him, if we hope to experience the freedom and life-mastery Christ offers.

The first step begins with understanding that the black horse is a composition of lies, unique to each of us, that we accept as truth. Whatever the lie, it produces toxic emotions, like fear and anger, that drive the black horse—and us—to all forms of destructive behaviors.

I'm not talking about bold-faced lies. Those sorts of deceptions are easy to ignore or dismiss. On the contrary, the lies that define the dark horse are entrenched within us, usually connected to our deepest wounds as men. This is what makes them so easy to believe and the prospect of dismissal so nonsensical. They are based in reality, only a warped and twisted version. From our childhood, we have subconsciously compiled half-truths and false evidence to construct a story of our existence that defines our reality. This story is the window through which we view the world.

From this hard won vantage point of self-discovery, we must come to see that the lies we believe, and the fears they trigger, often pose a threat only in our imagination. Because there is no actual peril, there is no cause for fear and a host of other inflamed emotions that drive our worst behaviors.

THE LIES WE BELIEVE

Perhaps you're wondering what this has to do with meeting your wife's deepest needs. Here's the connection. When a man is uncaring towards his wife, in thought or deed, his actions are ultimately spurred by a lie that has distorted how he thinks and feels about her.

Confronting these lies isn't easy, but it is every man's marital—and spiritual—duty. Those who seek to love their wife sacrificially, as Christ loves the church, must *fight* for the truth. This is because truth and love are wedded. Love cannot exist without truth. What I mean is this: We can't love our wife as God intends when what we think and feel about her is based upon lies. And it will be a fight. These lies are ingrained in our brains. They are unquestioned in our thinking.

One common lie sounds like this: *If I can't have what I want—beauty, and the respect and intimacy that go with it—I will be unfulfilled and insignificant.* It's easy for men to believe such lies because they intrinsically want to possess what is beautiful. In fact, the possession of beauty is central to how they define their masculinity.

> *Every man has subscribed to the lie that says the possession and enjoyment of beauty is my most important need.*

If that's the case, some men reason that they must possess and enjoy a beautiful woman to actualize their masculinity. If they don't, they will be suppressing who they are at their core—their manhood.

Of course, this lie is often combined with a second lie that says: *Because God won't meet my needs, I must meet them myself.* This is an obvious distortion of the truth. God *will* meet your needs (Philippians 4:19). And even if he doesn't meet them in the precise way you want, your manhood won't suffer. You'll still be strong because your identity is rooted in Christ (Galatians 2:20; 2 Corinthians 5:17). This reality cannot change. It is the truth.[48]

The lies that contradict this distort a man's thinking and cause his emotions to spiral out of control. He may become convinced his wife can't or won't meet his needs. He may think she's impossible to live with. Such lie-based thinking poisons his emotions and spurs the black horse, causing it to race across the field, pulling the white horse and chariot behind him. In a moment, a man's best qualities and dreams are dragged behind a lie-induced fear that is leading him where, in his true self, he would never go—towards every type of destructive behavior.

You Must Control the Black Horse

While the black horse is within you, it doesn't define you. You are the charioteer. In Christ, you have the power to reject lies, correct false thinking, and master your run-away emotions. The black horse doesn't have to take you and your life where you don't want to go.

To control him, you must identify the lies that empower him. But beware. Attaining such insight will take much prayer and self-reflection, in addition to one or two transparent relationships, such as with a trusted friend, pastor, or counselor. And if a lie has habitually triggered your fears and driven your behavior, it will take time to weaken its power over you. But each time you dispel it, its grip will be further loosened. As mentioned earlier in this book, medical science tells us when we change our thinking, from negative and lie-based to positive and truth-based, our tendency to think those same negative thoughts diminishes. The destructive thoughts literally vanish from our brain and are replaced with healthy ones. You have the ability to determine whether your thoughts are based on love and truth or fear and lies.

The apostle Paul put it this way, "We demolish arguments and every pretension that sets itself up against the knowledge of God, and we take captive every thought to make it obedient to Christ" (2 Corinthians 10:5 NIV).

The apostle is saying that through Christ, you have the power to dispel lies and control your thoughts and feelings for your wife.[49] You do this by realizing the Lord Jesus Christ stands in the chariot beside you. The moment fear and lies run away, Christ's hands will wrap around yours, infusing you with power so you can pull back lies and fear and release truth and love.

Jesus is the source of your spiritual strength. When you're living in alignment with him,[1] you will experience his power and use it to love your wife sacrificially.

---

1 In my book, *The Jesus Experiment*, I talk about how we can align our feelings, thoughts, words, and deeds with Jesus and, in the process, release his power in our lives.

MEDITATE UPON REGAINING CONTROL OF THE BLACK HORSE

Find a quiet place where you will be undisturbed for ten minutes. Sit in a comfortable chair and close your eyes. Imagine standing in a chariot with Jesus at your side. Two horses hitched side by side stand before you, a black one on the left and a white one on the right. Your hands hold the reins attached to the bridle of each horse—giving you control over the animals. Smell the country air. Notice the heat of the sun on your back and the cool breeze against your face. Feel the smooth texture of the reins in your hands.

Now flick the reins and shout a command. The horses begin trotting across an open field with you following behind. As you enjoy the beauty of the day, recall the one thing about your wife that most bothers you—the one behavior, habit, or trait that rubs you the wrong way. Perhaps she has saddled on more weight and doesn't seem to care. Maybe she talks to you disrespectfully in front of your children and friends. Perhaps she's lost interest in sex. Whatever it is, bring to mind the thoughts and feelings associated with this particular struggle.

As you do, the black horse pulls away with the white horse and chariot in tow. Racing across the field, you look beyond the horses and realize you're speeding toward a dark forest. You intuitively sense you can't slip through unharmed. If you continue on this course, your chariot will be destroyed along with your life and everything you love.

While you consider this terrifying thought, Jesus leans over and speaks into your ear, "What lies spurred him?"

You quickly run through the possibilities and realize you've believed numerous lies.

- *God won't take care of me. I'm on my own.*
- *I must have what I want or else deny my manhood.*
- *My wife doesn't care about me. No one does.*
- *My wife can no longer meet my needs. But another woman could.*
- *No one is looking out for me. I need to look out for myself, not my wife.*
- *Other women are much more attractive than my wife.*
- *I'll start serving her when she starts serving me.*

The black horse is running faster and pulling harder. The forest is growing bigger and more ominous. Destruction is moments away. You can't can rein him in. And then again you hear the Lord's voice. "Expose these lies to truth." Instantly you tell yourself:

- *God is faithful and will meet my every need.*
- *My manhood isn't dependent upon getting what I want.*
- *Serving my wife strengthens my manhood.*
- *My wife loves me and I love her.*
- *Another woman won't meet my needs better than my wife.*

- *God called me to love and protect my wife.*
- *My wife is beautiful.*
- *I've committed my life to serving her.*[50]

With the forest quickly approaching, you hear the Lord shout, "You are the charioteer. With my power, pull the reins of the black horse and release those of the white horse. Restrict lies and fears; release love and truth."

While he speaks, you feel his warm, rough hands wrap around yours. You sense his supernatural strength surging within you. You command the imaginary gatekeeper of your mind, *I reject these lying thoughts. Don't let them back into my mind. If one sneaks in, let me know so I can kick it out again.*[51]

You feel the power of the lies weakening as the black horse slows to a walk and you regain control. Toxic emotions wash away and in their place, you're overcome with a sense of joy, peace, love and compassion. You confidently turn the horses toward a low grass hill in the distance.

As you near, you notice your wife sitting on a stretched out blanket with a picnic basket at her side and your dog standing nearby. She tosses a ball past you, down the hill, and the dog bounds over the grass in pursuit. Your children are playing nearby, and you see their smiles and hear their laughter. You approach your wife and stop the chariot. She stands and looks at you with immense pride on her face. After securing the reins, you climb out and embrace her. While holding her in your arms, you whisper in her ear, "I love you forever."

AFTERTHOUGHT

The first command God gave man was to "Be fruitful and increase in number; fill the earth and subdue it" (Genesis 1:28, NIV). In order to help man fulfill that command, God gave him a powerful sexual appetite. This driving force can be directed toward good or evil, love or hate. It can compel a man to seek gratification without regard for others, destroying his life and those he loves.

Or that same energy can propel a man to love his wife as Christ loved the church— sacrificially, with everything inside of him, cultivating life in his family and friends. The choice is yours— with the power of Christ, you have the

strength to choose love. You have the power to choose good.

At the beginning of this book, I promised that the lessons you would learn in these pages would lead to life transformation. I hope by understanding why naked women look so good, you have found this to be true. I hope you more deeply appreciate the mystery of sexual magnetism between a man and woman. And I hope what you've learned will guide you, step by step, in the ways you can meet your wife's deepest needs for the rest of your lives.

Why Naked Women Look so Good Review Table

Chapter	Reason	Wife's Need	Your Actions
1	Mystery	Viewed with wonder	See and praise her wonder
2	Hidden Beauty	Affirmed for sexiness	Praise her sexiness
3	Companionship	Best Friend	Love, listen, forgive, and have fun
4	Relational Wholeness	To Complete You	Express how she completes you
5	Her Glory	Understanding	Ask questions and praise her
6	Intimacy	Intimacy	Pray together
7	Sexual Playmate	Meet her Sexual Needs	Go Slow
8	Bridle	Relational Security	Talk Commitment

ABOUT THE AUTHOR (AND OTHERS)

Bill Perkins is an author and speaker. He has written or collaborated on more than twenty books and has addressed audiences across the United States and internationally. Bill pastored in Texas and Oregon for 24 years and is currently the president of Million Mighty Men and the Jesus Experiment Cross Walk. Bill and his wife, Cindy, have three grown sons, two grandchildren, a Chihuahua and a Goldendoodle. They live in West Linn, Oregon. Bill enjoys working out, reading, cooking, scuba diving and biking with Cindy.

Robert Falcone is a full-time designer, doodler, husband and father. Robert and his wife, Stephani, have a daughter, a son, and two dogs. They live and play in West Linn, Oregon where they enjoy the stunning and vast wilderness of the Pacific Northwest. Whether he's on the coast or a mountain, you'll often find Robert hiking, running, skiing, kayaking or biking.

Time to clear the stage—
turn on the spotlight—
and let my friends take a bow.

Paul Perkins, my attorney son, spent untold hours editing. His fingerprints are on every page and his insights and additions make it much better. If he had agreed, I would have made him the co-author. Please give Paul a standing ovation.

Robert Falcone and his wife Stephanie were part of the focus group that read the book and then gave helpful suggestions. As Robert and I were talking one night I told him I thought the book needed stick figures. He raised his hand and volunteered to do the drawings. By the way, I was Robert's soccer coach when he was a boy and officiated at his wedding when he was a man. We had a lot of fun figuring out what ideas warranted a stick figure. One proof of Robert's wisdom is the amazing woman he married. Please take a bow, Robert and Stephanie.

While Cindy, my wife, didn't read and reread the book until it was almost finished, her insights made a huge difference. She spotted flaws nobody else had seen. Her eye for detail and ability to see logical inconsistencies tightened the message and give it focus. Now I must get her a pair of red boots. Put your hands together for my wonderful wife.

Bonne Steffen, my editor, took what we all thought was a good manuscript and showed us how to make it better. And when I kept sending back revisions, she cheerfully edited again and again. Bonne, please take a bow.

Ed and Barb Cox were part of the focus group that looked at an early version of the book and shared some thoughts that pointed out weaknesses and tweaked some ideas to improve them. Please give them a round of applause.

Nelson Larson and I became friends when he fell in love with Jenny Bellone, the daughter of my former neighbor and long-time friend, Ernie Bellone. Nelson and Jenny are now married and he's a professional soccer coach in the Portland, Oregon area. He loved all of the book but one chapter. In fact he disliked it so much he urged me to throw it out. His comment caused me to rewrite that chapter no less than thirty times. For an honest and helpful critique, please put your hands together for Nelson.

My publisher, Bryan Heathman, called me after he

had heard me speak at a men's conference and asked if I had any book ideas. I mentioned the title of this book and he wanted to know more. I appreciate Bryan's willingness to allow his publishing house to give birth to an idea I've had for fifteen years. As the spotlight hits Bryan, you'll see his wife, DeeDee, at his side. She is the mind behind the cover and the layout of the book. Give them both a round of applause.

OTHER BOOKS BY BILL PERKINS

Available at Your Online Retail Stores

Men know all about their need for sexual purity. What they want is a plan that will enable them to attain it. In the midst of a culture that shouts 'Sex!' from every corner, men need a friend to talk honestly about how to master lust and achieve control over this crucial area of their lives. Bill Perkins details a proven biblical strategy for sexual integrity. He shows men how to achieve a purity that will flow from their relationship with God and strengthen their self-respect, the sanctity of their marriage, and the security of their families. Perkins unfolds a three-part plan that will lead men to victory. Updated to address current needs and cultural trends, *When Good Men Are Tempted* includes the latest information on Internet pornography. It also features 'Take Action' strategic steps and questions suitable for individual reflection or discussion in small groups.

If you loved *The Purpose-Driven Life* and *One Month to Live*, then you'll love *The Jesus Experiment*. Popular author and speaker Bill Perkins challenges you to spend twelve weeks discovering what it really means to live like Jesus. More than a book, it's an invitation for you to try becoming like him in your feelings, thoughts, words, and deeds. Each week, you'll focus on a different aspect of Jesus' life, including how he faced his fears, how he talked with God, and how he helped others. As you examine your own life in light of the Lord's, you'll be amazed at how your mind and heart will change to more closely reflect his.

The story of David's "mighty men" (primarily found in 2 Samuel 23) drives this challenging and encouraging book for Christian men. The mighty men weren't drafted into David's army because of their impressive resumes. They were broken men who, given an opportunity to achieve greatness, responded like champions. In *Six Battles Every Man Must Win*, popular author and speaker Bill Perkins uses the story to illustrate the six battles David's men fought, and men today must win, to become powerful and effective warriors in God's kingdom.

With startling frankness, Bill Perkins offers life-changing wisdom to help men find true freedom in Christ. Perkins shatters six man-made rules that sound good on the outside, but often keep men from reaching their full potential. He shows how breaking these taboos can help you break free to become the man that God created you to be. The Rule of Passivity, Never Get In a Fight, The Rule of Playing it Safe, Never Risk It All, The Rule of Perseverance, Never Give Up, The Rule of Independence, Never Ask For Help, The Rule of Restraint, Never Lose Your Cool, The Rule of Impressing Others, and Never Look Stupid.

Be honest, guys: Have you ever made a foolish or harmful decision when angry? Have you ever said or done something in the heat of the moment that you wish you could take back? Or do you tend to keep your anger hidden, choosing to bury the feeling and hoping it just goes away? No matter how often you get angry, or how you express it, Bill Perkins (best-selling author of *When Good Men Are Tempted* and *6 Rules Every Man Must Break*) has written this book to provide you with the insight and biblical strategy you need to deal with this crucial issue (as well as help for the women in your life who are walking through the anger with you). Illustrated with research-based statistics and real-life stories of men who have successfully dealt with anger, *When Good Men Get Angry* explores the foundations of anger--what it is, where it comes from, how Jesus expressed it, and how the new and good man in you can control it.

Endnotes:

[1] I don't mean I had an ongoing problem looking through the window. I mean that unless I let my grass die or removed the temptation, I would face it every night. The impending temptation was the "problem" I faced. In my book *When Good Men are Tempted*, I tell the entire story . . . what I said to my wife when she asked why it took so long to turn on the water, what I told—or didn't tell—my accountability partners the next morning, and how I dealt with my "problem." By the way, that "problem" led to the publication of *When Good Men are Tempted*, *When Young Men are Tempted*, and over a decade later, this book. It's fascinating that a single temptation and how we deal with it can affect our lives for good or evil. Sometimes what we're most ashamed of is where God will meet us with his grace. He will use our weakness to help others because his strength in our weakness gives hope to others with a similar weakness. Where we are weak, he is strong. God's desire is for our identity to no longer rest on our weakness but on his strength in our weakness (2 Corinthians 12:7-10).

[2] Many of these principles are found in my book, *When Good Men are Tempted*. Published by Zondervan, 1997, revised 2007, Grand Rapids, Michigan.

[3] *Brain Basics: Understanding Sleep*, National Institute of Neurological Disorders and Strokes (NIH Publication

No.06-3440-c), *available at* http://www.ninds.nih.gov/disorders/brain_basics/understanding_sleep.htm

[4] Ibid.

[5] MomGrind, "Women And Body Image: Ten Disturbing Facts." You can access the article at http://momgrind.com/2009/01/28/women-body-image/

[6] Carolyn Leaf, Ph.D., *Who Switched off My Brain?* (Nashville: Thomas Nelson, 2009). This book explains in understandable terms how the brain works and how our thinking shapes our emotions. If this subject interests you, I would encourage you to get a copy. It's a short book and will likely change the way you think and feel. It certainly gives credence to the exercises in this book which urge you to think positive thoughts about your wife. I came across Dr. Leaf's book as I was living the Jesus Experiment—*The Jesus Experiment* is a book I recently published about living an experiment to see if Jesus truly gives abundant life. As I practiced the spiritual disciplines laid out in the book, I overcame a fear that had been threatening me with depression. The switch in my thinking and the subsequent improvement in my emotions, from fear to joy, were so radical and long lasting that I wondered what was going on in my brain. Reading Dr. Leaf's book gave me a scientific understanding of the miracle God's Spirit was doing in my life. I'm thankful to her for some amazing insights. Since you're a devoted reader—devoted enough to

read footnotes—I want to give you a heads-up. The chariot story in the last chapter was used by God to enable me to get control of this fear. When you read that story, you'll now have the backstory. I know God can improve your feelings for your wife as you manage your thoughts.

[7] I learned in the early years of my marriage that I couldn't simultaneously think a negative and positive thought about my wife. Let me ask you, what are you seeking to accomplish with the negative thoughts about your wife? Are you stoking anger so you'll be more forceful when you talk with her? Are you seeking justification for distancing yourself from her? I'm not judging, just curious. Can you think of anything good that would come from such thinking? Probably not. The fact is, negative thoughts will poison you. But you can stop the flow of toxins and replace them with life-giving chemicals by changing the way you think.

[8] Every man and woman has an emotional "love bank." This means that all of your words and actions either withdraw from or deposit into your wife's emotional love bank. You want to be sure you're making more deposits than withdrawals. The exercises in this book are designed to help you make those deposits.

[9] It occurred to me tonight that as your wife hears your praise and reviews it in her mind, she is restoring her mind and creating healing emotions. Your words are

powerful. Solomon acknowledged this when he said, "The tongue of the wise brings healing" (Proverbs 12:18).

[10] Unlike horses, Great Danes have weak backs and should never be ridden. But children didn't know that and they would beg to climb on his back.

[11] You can watch this classic on YouTube at http://www.youtube.com/watch?v=sShMA85pv8M. Or Google, "Who's on First".

[12] Tim Allen, *Don't Stand Too Close to a Naked Man* (New York: Hyperion, 1994), 5354.

[13] I'm not sure who originally said this, but I first heard it from my friend Ed Cox. He and his wife, Barb, were part of a focus group that read an unfinished version of this book and offered some helpful suggestions.

[14] *The American Heritage Dictionary of the English Language*, Fourth Edition published by Houghton Mifflin Harcourt Publishing Company, assessed on the Internet using Master Writer.

[15] You might think this forgetfulness only occurs after many years of marriage. Such isn't always the case. Cindy and I had only been married a few months when each of us said if we had it to do over again we would not have married each other. Fortunately, God's grace

restored our love and we weathered those turbulent months and emerged with a stronger relationship than before.

[16] All of us have been touched by divorce in some way. And while a lifelong union is God's ideal, if a marriage ends in divorce and a man or woman remarries, the new marriage is now the one that should last a lifetime.

[17] Mark Driscoll, *Real Marriage* (Nashville: Thomas Nelson, 2012), 1941.

[18] John Gottman and Nan Silver, *The Seven Principles for Making Marriage Work* (New York: Three Rivers Press, 1999), 17.

[19] Ibid., 1920.

[20] I can't say enough about the importance of maintaining a positive tone of voice when you speak with your wife. Here's an experiment that will show you what I mean. If you've got a dog, speak harshly and say, "You're a good dog." Your words are affirming but your tone is gruff. How would you expect your dog respond? He would cower, right? Likewise, your wife is more responsive to how you say something than what you say. She hears your voice tone more clearly than your words. If she says you're not listening, be careful that both your words and tone are affirming and non-defensive when you respond. Of course, you should

always seek to maintain a positive not judgmental or angry tone when speaking with your wife.

[21] Anger management is an issue for many men. I'm not suggesting that all anger can be quickly dealt with in an evening. If this is a subject you'd like to work through in more detail, I would urge you to get a copy of my book, *When Good Men Get Angry*.

[22] This was not a hard and fast rule. We tried to resolve disputes before going to sleep. But if we were tired, we would sleep and deal with it the next day. The point is, we sought to process anger quickly to protect ourselves from bitterness.

[23] *New Love: A Short Shelf Life*, The New York Times, December 2, 2012, *available at* http://mobile.nytimes.com/2012/12/02/opinion/sunday/new-love-a-short-shelf-life.xml?single=1

[24] Shalom speaks not only of peace, but of being well, happy and healthy. Strong's Hebrew Lexicon, 7965. You can access this lexicon online. *The Online Etymology Dictionary*, 2010, says the word also means "completeness." *Online Etymology Dictionary*. You can find this at http://dictionary.reference.com/browse/shalom

[25] C.S. Lewis, *Mere Christianity*, You can access the quote at www.goodreads.com.

[26] I'm sometimes asked if I believe there is only "one" person in the world for each individual to marry. I would say, "No," in the sense that we have the free will to select from many people the "one" we will marry. There are probably many people who would make a good match. On the other hand, I would say, "Yes," in the sense that God rules over everything and there is nothing outside his plan. So the woman I chose to marry must have been the "one" he intended me to marry since he is sovereign. This too is a great mystery.

[27] I realize this statement invites misconstruing. So for the record, I'm not saying a woman's identity is wrapped up in finding a man. I grew up with four, count them four, sisters and no brothers. My sisters are strong women who beat me up and protected me from bullies. I appreciate both the strength and tenderness of women. With this statement, I'm referring to the desire for male companionship that resides in the heart of even the strongest woman.

[28] This surfaces the problem of women who had either an absent or an abusive father. Where do they go to gain a sense of identity? Many women have suffered deep wounds by their father and it has greatly affected how they view themselves. They need their husband to assure them of their value and the important role they play in his life.

[29] Mike Mason, *The Mystery of Marriage* (Portland, OR.: Multnomah Press, 1985), 115. This is one of the best

books on marriage I've read. It's been out a while but is well worth reading.

30 C. H. Spurgeon commented on this in a sermon (No. 3120) delivered on November 26, 1908, at New Park Street Chapel, Southwark. I accessed it at http://www. spurgeon.org/sermons/3120.htm.

31 Two of my focus group readers said they thought some of the end-of-the-chapter questions and suggestions were cheesy. But then both of them spontaneously said, "But women really like this kind of stuff." So if you also think they're cheesy, you've got company. Cheesy or not, your wife will probably like them.

32 I'm speaking of a woman who willingly undresses for a man. Not an abusive situation where a man forces a woman to undress against her will.

33 Ibid., MomGrind.

34   See   http://www.dailymail.co.uk/tvshowbiz/ article-1265676/Britney-Spears-releases-airbrushed-images-digitally-altered-versions.html.

35 Words and music by Skip Ewing and Kenny Chesney. Copyright © 1999 Acuff Rose Music, Inc. (BMI), 65 Music Square West, Nashville, TN 37203. All rights reserved.

[36] I considered using a different word than "animalistic." But I think it fits because it describes creatures who engage in sex for gratification without a basis of intimacy.

[37] I'm not writing this book to help you overcome sexual compulsions and addictions. This is already a subject I've written about in my book *When Good Men are Tempted*, which offers helpful insights and strategies. Here I'm identifying a common barrier to marital intimacy that can be overcome with effort and God's grace.

[38] S. Craig Glickman, *A Song for Lovers*, (Downers Grove, IL.: InterVarsity Press, 1976), 21.

[39] Ibid., 2425

[40] It's true that Paul is now driving with "grace." However, during the writing of this book he ran his car into a concrete barricade. He wondered why the line of cars was going so slow and not using the right lane. He soon found out. No worries, though, since both he and the concrete barricade escaped uninjured. The car didn't fare as well. He considers the collision a wake-up call from God that, as he approaches his wedding day, he must put behaviors such as reckless driving that defined his thirty-one years of singleness behind him, since he will soon be responsible for not only his life, but for his wife's too.

[41] Women go through different sexual stages during the course of their lives. If you would like more information, I would encourage you to visit www.womensknows.com. You'll find an excellent article there entitled, "Sexual Stages of Women." I mention this because what works best for your wife will depend, in part, on where she happens to be in terms of her sexual stage of life. An article like this might help you better understand your wife and her sexual needs.

[42] Shaunti Feldhahn, *For Women Only,* (Colorado Springs: Multnomah Books, 2006), p. 181-182, large print. If you're a woman, I would urge you to read this book. She skillfully addresses this sensitive subject so you'll understand your husband's need for you to try to look your best. Plus, she gives excellent coaching tips.

[43] There are circumstances in which cosmetic surgery is a wise choice. I'm not passing judgment on those who elect to have such surgeries, just pointing out the risk.

[44] Peter wasn't saying women are emotionally or spiritually weaker than men. He was saying they are *physically* weaker. Instead of using brute force to overpower his weaker wife, a husband should seek to understand and love her. At the time Peter wrote this letter, women had few legal rights and were often mistreated. The apostle stood up to this injustice and demanded men live with their wives in a tender and understanding way.

[45] Wendy Plump, "A Roomful of Yearning and Regret," *New York Times* (December 9, 2010). The illustration of the bomb was taken from this article. It's the best article I've read on the emotional damage wrought by an affair.

[46] Jennifer Steinhauer, *Studies Find Big Benefits in Marriage, New York Times* (April 10, 1995).

[47] See note 30 above.

[48] Just as a page finds its identity within the covers of a book, so a man's identity is in Christ. The placement of a book, on a shelf or a table, doesn't affect the identity of the page. Similarly, our manhood doesn't depend on whether or not we get our way. It's rests in Christ.

[49] While Paul doesn't explicitly say our feelings can be controlled, it's a logical outcome of controlling our thoughts. The reference to "our wife" isn't stated by Paul in this passage either. I mention this by way of application.

[50] You might try reading these two lists every day for a couple weeks to train yourself to combat lies with truth. Or, you could make your own list and read it daily for a while.

[51] I often feel a negative emotion before I understand what thought triggered it. For that reason whenever I

have a negative feeling toward my wife I try to identify if a lie birthed it. If so, I've found that telling myself—the imaginary gatekeeper—to keep that thought out of my mind works very well. I used to struggle with a thought and get mad at myself for thinking in such a way. Instead of struggling, just tell your gatekeeper to remove the thought and not let it in again. If it sneaks in, kick it out as soon as you identify it. If you'll consistently do this, the thought will literally disappear from your brain. For more details on how this works, check out Carolyn Leaf's book noted under footnote six.